© Daniel Owusu

Momtaza Mehri is an award-winning poet and essayist working across research, criticism, education, and radio. She is a former Young People's Poet Laureate for London and winner of the 2019 Manchester Writing Prize. She has also been a Poet-in-Residence at Homerton College, University of Cambridge. Her writing has featured in the *Guardian*, POETRY, Wasafiri, ArtReview, frieze, and across the BBC. *Bad Diaspora Poems* is the winner of an Eric Gregory Award and the 2023 Forward Prize for Best First Collection.

Praise for *Bad Diaspora Poems*

Winner of the Forward Prize for Best First Collection

Winner of the Sky Arts Award for Poetry

Winner of a Somerset Maugham Award

Finalist for the Sunday Times Young Writer of the Year Award

Shortlisted for the Books Are My Bag Readers Awards

'Mehri brings unflinching discursive skills to verse that melds criticism, autobiography and essay while still achieving a crisp sonic momentum characteristic of lyric poetry ... Hers is a dazzling voice that refuses to speak from a podium'
Guardian, Poetry Book of the Month

'Mehri's work is not just politically vital but poetically alive'
Sunday Times, Books of the Year

'Sensitive, tender, measured, hopeful ... *Bad Diaspora Poems* is a classic'
Magma

'An exceptional debut collection that reinvigorates ideas around diaspora, migration and home. Wide-ranging and ambitious, her poetry shimmers with erudition and linguistic exquisiteness, while also having an emotional heart. Drawing on global cultures, Mehri is a truly transnational poet of the twenty-first century whose words pulsate out into the world-at-large'
Bernardine Evaristo, author of *Girl, Woman, Other*

'A poet like Momtaza Mehri comes only once in a generation. Mehri is a writer of refined insight, audacious imagination and artful technicality – a genius. *Bad Diaspora Poems* is a feat, its scope of movement both in time and geography is immense, you are swallowed into its voyage. This is an essential collection in the Black diasporic discourse'
Caleb Femi, author of *Poor*

'Momtaza Mehri's debut collection refuses the presentist and egoist pitfalls of the lyric and avoids the reductive slipstreams and intellectual constraints of identity politics. With her dexterity of tone and breadth of reference, her sense of history and geopolitical scope, Mehri develops a unique new poetic, rich in its connectivity and attentiveness. *Bad Diaspora Poems*' satirical insight and humane outlook are energising, radical and remarkable'
Jack Underwood, author of *A Year in the New Life*

'One of the most unique and striking poetry debuts'
Raymond Antrobus, author of *The Perseverance*

'Momtaza Mehri is in the advance party of a daring new turn in global anglophone poetry. Though to say 'new' doesn't do full justice to her innovation; the word implies adherence to tastes or fashion but what we have in *Bad Diaspora Poems* is something rarer altogether: the poems collected here, being poems with a timeless sense of style, are destined to last even as they speak so incisively to our present moment'
Kayo Chingonyi, author of *Kumukanda*

'Masterful . . . The poems gathered here take nothing for granted. They revel in the slippages of belonging and identity and strive for something greater, something closer to a revolutionary kind of love'
Victoria Adukwei Bulley, author of *Quiet*

'This collection feels special, even in the hands, a total privilege to read. Mehri is an incredible poet, thinker, seer; ridiculously intelligent, irreverent, and with the ability to laugh, bitterly, in the face of some of the saddest personal and world history. Her unique poetic eye cuts through everything'
Rachel Long, author of *My Darling from the Lions*

'Momtaza Mehri is a groundbreaking new voice. Raw and sophisticated, *Bad Diaspora Poems* is a gloriously rich mosaic, offering insights into our planet's increasingly exiled populations, the plight of refugees, and a passionate longing for the homeland'
Pascale Petit, author of *Mama Amazonica*

MOMTAZA MEHRI

Bad Diaspora Poems

VINTAGE

1 3 5 7 9 10 8 6 4 2

Vintage is part of the Penguin Random House group of companies

Vintage, Penguin Random House UK, One Embassy Gardens,
8 Viaduct Gardens, London SW11 7BW

penguin.co.uk/vintage
global.penguinrandomhouse.com

First published in Vintage in 2025
First published in hardback by Jonathan Cape in 2023

Copyright © Momtaza Mehri 2023

The moral right of the author has been asserted

Penguin Random House values and supports copyright. Copyright fuels creativity, encourages diverse voices, promotes freedom of expression and supports a vibrant culture. Thank you for purchasing an authorised edition of this book and for respecting intellectual property laws by not reproducing, scanning or distributing any part of it by any means without permission. You are supporting authors and enabling Penguin Random House to continue to publish books for everyone. No part of this book may be used or reproduced in any manner for the purpose of training artificial intelligence technologies or systems. In accordance with Article 4(3) of the DSM Directive 2019/790, Penguin Random House expressly reserves this work from the text and data mining exception.

Printed and bound in Great Britain by Clays Ltd, Elcograf S.p.A.

The authorised representative in the EEA is Penguin Random House Ireland,
Morrison Chambers, 32 Nassau Street, Dublin D02 YH68

A CIP catalogue record for this book is available from the British Library

ISBN 9781529922561

Penguin Random House is committed to a sustainable future for our business, our readers and our planet. This book is made from Forest Stewardship Council® certified paper.

This collection was written within sight of the Mediterranean Sea

Contents

1830s

Conditionals — 3

By Such Honorifics, You Attempt to Summon the Old Country You Have Never Seen — 4

A Few Facts We Hesitantly Know to Be Somewhat True — 5

Rimbaud in Harar — 6

Harar in Rimbaud — 8

Reciprocity is a Two-way Street — 9

Somewhere in Napoli, Sometime in May — 13

1936

From a Distance, Anteo Zamboni Glimpses the White Horse — 17

From a Distance, Anteo Zamboni Glimpses the Ageing Poet — 19

The Flower of the Thousand and One Nights — 21

Postcard from Castelporziano: Rare Scenes of a Poet Caught in a State of Glorified Impotence — 24

1960

Preludes — 31

An Age Until Lunch Break, An Agony at Mogadishu's Gamal Abdel Nasser School — 32

Gradations — 33

On Memory as Molasses as Muscle as Miasma — 34

You Will Never Tell Your Daughters — 36

You Will Deny It All	37
You Will Heave Your Body	38

1977? / 1987? / 1991?

Procession	41
Later	42
Wink Wink	43
Iqama	44
This Little, This Late	45
Untitled	46
Sufficiently Memorable Password Recovery Questions for the Refugee Parent	47

Year Zero

Fledglings	51
Fluke by Any Other Name is a Flight Number	53
I Scream, You Scream, We All Scream for Ice Cream	54
Brief Dialogue Between the Self-declared East African Micronations of Regent Park Estate (Toronto) & Regent's Park Estate (London)	56
Übertragung	58
The Apocalypse Will Taste Like Concentrated Grape Juice	60
The Polyphonic Urgencies of Paltalk 2.0	61
A Violet Coagulation of Dispersals	62
Balcony Dispatches, 2002	67

2003–present

First Sight	71
Landing	72

Delete as Appropriate	74
The Plural Possible	75
Apricot Season	78
Dunyā	79

2020

The Native Informant Describes a Reading to Her Friends in the Ends	83
A Tableau of Aspiration or Franklin Sitting on the Solitary Garden Deckchair in 1973's *A Charlie Brown Thanksgiving*	85
A Guest Takes Off Her Shoes	89
If You Call Me Brother, Am I Yours?	91
Muddied Commitments	93
Glory Be to the Gang Gang Gang	100
Akhis & Afterthoughts	101
Bad Diaspora Poem	104
Acknowledgements	111
Notes	113

1830s

Fugitives settle in the Jubba Valley, forming communities of runaways. The forest is sovereign.

Somali nomad. Italian planter. British administrator.

The first wave resists all. The first wave is friendless.

Conditionals

If we love the same things, that makes us friends.
If we hate the same things, that makes us friends.

If we dream in the same language, that makes us friends.
If we flinch from the same hands, that makes us friends.

If we eat breakfast before ten, that makes us friends.
If we agree on the same lies, that makes us countrymen.

By Such Honorifics, You Attempt to Summon the Old Country You Have Never Seen

Flat wishbone
Depository of guilt
Tally of defences
Redemption arc
Recreational facility
Excuse for a personality
Get Out of Jail Free card
Father's belt
Ideological crutch
Cartographical mirage
Chosen affliction
Spilt milk
Pool of amnesia
Extreme sport
Terminal psychodrama
Unfinished eulogy
Crowded abattoir
Nursery of martyrs
Pitiless receptacle
Basin of platitudes
Lovable bastard
Unreliable host
Enduring headache
Bad joke
O,

A Few Facts We Hesitantly Know to Be Somewhat True

I. *I am uneasy thinking that you may be attracted to the tragedy of me* George Jackson wrote & he could have easily been talking about lovers or prisoners or poets or refugees or all at once or none at all. All deserve love letters.

II. We are one people of one stock of one language of one religion of one coast of one desire.

III. Whatever helps you sleep at night won't let you rest by day.

IV. Richard Burton learnt Somali in the laps of women. In this way, we are monstrously alike.

V. Equilibrium is not a destination you can relocate to.

VI. Castro and Barre met in 1977. A private encounter with no witnesses. Some say Barre pointed to the map and said that anywhere one of us stood was ours, all ours. We just had to take it.

VII. Our proverbs are often defence mechanisms.

VIII. You can't call us Horners and seriously expect us not to be hard-headed.

IX. Art is something we do when the war ends.

X. Even when no one dies on the journey, something always does.

Rimbaud in Harar

'As for Harar, there is no consulate, no post office, no roads; you go there by camel, and you live exclusively with negroes. But you are free there, and the climate is good.'

— Arthur Rimbaud's letter to his mother, November 1890

Spat out into a dhow's empty belly,
you trembled like some abandoned animal.
Failed revolutionaries mewl like alley cats.
Who can stand to hear such loss?
Such bottomless need. You fled on your heels.

Roamed this licked throng of ports. Red sea beckons.
Bellows. Every bad boy deserves a third act.
Ardennes, aback. Aden, ahead.
The gulf is an itch. You are a tidy apparition.
Your cotton shirt is a thin membrane.

So sublimely particular, that lump in your throat
will persist all the way to Zeila.
Twenty days and twenty nights. A torn belt of desert.
Stars like loose teeth to be counted.
Whoever will die will die.

Old men stretch their shining calves.
Offer you a single ostrich feather. Keepsakes.
Your pockets are filled with rice grains.
Here, you have come to feel something again.
For the last, forsaken time.

Rimbaud in Harar

Opposite the crumbling masjid, sandflies rub hands,
perform their ablutions on balcony rims.
Each dawn brings its swell of prayer.
Your mouth, encrusted with salt,
will learn the shape of new vowels.

You are a shower of impulse.
The house girl will help with that.
Youth trickles like an evening on the verandah.
No peace like this peace of hyenas,
this reverie of banana trees, your netted shadow

against the city's walls. Five gates.
Don't mistake yourself for one.
Europe is still your holster on the hip.
The Seine is your inky laugh line.
Your scrawlings still decorate Luxor's columns.

Man-child dervish of retired derangements.
Who can deny you your past?
Frenzied darling of transcendent filth,
of brief springs when poets are reborn
as swaggering policemen, of epochs redoubling

in waves, in the honeyed delirium of revolt.
There, you will always be young.
Always be our preferred season of provocation.
A smear of a boy, rearranging your limbs
in the cramped bowels of a chambre de bonne.

As rapturously open as a gash.
Your fingers splayed against frosted glass.
Your face, a dish of milk.

Harar in Rimbaud

dried inkwell
gun fingers up
rebrand accordingly
trader
dog-killer
mercenary
spice-flogger
slave-driver
teetotal has-been
lounging expat
erratic teenage dream
reckless lice-seeker

summertime & the living is easy
your daddy's absent & your mama's sick
your old man boils seawater
somewhere in Algiers
he plants a tricolour
self-annihilation is a moving goalpost
find it in Africa
invariably Africa
motherless mother
melt
into the mutilation of its leaky cosmos

questions will be asked
you don't have to answer
settlers drink from reservoirs of goodwill
spit forth their catalogued observations
drowning
as they inspect

Reciprocity is a Two-way Street

> *'It isn't right to despise one's country.*
> *I don't deserve to be loved and left.'*
>
> — Faysal Cumar Mushteeg

Say you are reading Barthes, or rereading Barthes,
two acts which are hardly independent of each other.
Say it's *A Lover's Discourse* and you are all aflush,
your finger tracing the outline of flight,
Either woe or well-being, he writes,
sometimes I have a craving to be engulfed.
And even though this could mean anything,
you think you know what it means
to shiver with well-practised yearning.
Not for provincial beginnings, nor Moroccan boys,
but for lip-shaped crescent moons left on teacups.
An oil splash of a man with scarred hands.
In this poem, he doesn't have a name.
Your own dumb luck pools around your ankles.
We skirt around it. A kindness.
It disgusts you, the depth of this need,
like the slick walls of a well.
Your bones ache most when held.
Eventually, you'll have to stop impersonating a skimmed stone.
There are other ways of parting.

You annotate Barthes annotating Keats,
half in love with easeful Death.
Overidentify until you are light-headed.
Until you remember a hot, loud classroom.
Breathless Bluetooth blues, a free school meal in your belly,
the easy cruelty of teachers at under-performing schools,
so unlike their counterparts in the movies, so unlike
those loose-tied English teachers who promise you a world
so much bigger than this. So much easier than this.
With your prized set of highlighters, you mistake a poem for a blueprint.
First the Odes, then the Jane Campion film.
That night, you dreamt of lavender fields, bruised eyelids,
the shape of Rome's dying sunlight on a poet's grave.

> *Here lies One*
> *Whose name was Writ in Water.*

No name. No date. This was all Keats wanted.
Convinced they knew better, his friends contextualised their grief,
added the rest.

> *This Grave*
> *contains all that was Mortal,*
> *of a*
> *YOUNG ENGLISH POET,*
> *Who,*
> *on his Death Bed,*
> *in the Bitterness of his Heart,*
> *at the Malicious Power of his Enemies,*
> *Desired*
> *these Words to be engraven on his Tomb Stone*

You think of how casually our bodies are overruled by kin,
by blood, by heartaches disguised as homelands.
How you can count the years you have lived for yourself on one hand.
History is the hammer. You are the nail.
In another dream, your mother is barefoot and young,
wearing a scarf the colour of a wound.
By Fontana del Moro, a Moor adrift on a conch shell leans
over her shoulder. She unpeels her wet dress from her legs.
Unmoored, she laughs at this new country calling itself an old one.
These myths she tosses like rusty coins.
We don't dare dip our hands further than they can reach.
Her gold bracelets slide down the silk flags of her wrists.
Nightly, you strive to write an imprecise translation of this.
Arterial blood is theatrical, like the desire for a time before your time.
The world will not stop when you do, or even before.
Yes, being the one who survived, the one who made it to this side,
is a full-time job. But no one asked you to take it.
Diaspora is witnessing a murder without getting blood on your shirt.
Your body is the evidence of its absence.

Of course, there are other definitions.
Namely, a freshly scraped scalp,
a dome to your rock, the inevitability of fajr
and late-night texts.
Each lie about how good the exchange rate really was.
That time he cried telling you the story of why his family had left Sweden.
The image of a younger brother held underwater by wild-eyed classmates.
Definitions, like flags, lay claim to what has always existed.
For now, these will do. You can't speak for the future.
It barely speaks for you.
Pick a mask and ask him to wear it.
You only know love like this.
An interpretation you can't outrun.
A footnote haunting the page.

Somewhere in Napoli, Sometime in May

Door-knocker bears some devil's face.
A black tongue from beyond your known world.
Cloven-hoofed Pan, perhaps, or some other
wild-haired figure recognisable, at first,
only by your fist closing around its ears,
your letting go, then, the tremulous sound
of struck wood. Touch is vernacular.

Light decays. You let a stranger enter ahead of you.
Leave agape a space for your body to turn,
to step into this new life you have stalked
like an arsonist lingering at the scene of their obsession.

Young women like lamps in the sticky night.
A gaggle by the hot springs.
Stinking of bukhoor & defeat,
their linked arms a rope of tension.
Their dazed laughter arrives as dewdrops do.
Disappears by morning. Like them,
you have shrouded your past in folds of linen.
Tonight, you will bend like cranes, holding onto each other,
squeezing past your girlhood's slim ghosts.
Tittering down emptying streets named after fez-adorned soldiers.
You will wait for your giddy plans to fall apart
like a country
in your hands.

1936

Under the banner of a black flag, Africa Orientale Italiana bludgeons together a colony in the Horn.

Six governorates. One dream of expansion.

The people flee in all directions.

From a Distance,
Anteo Zamboni Glimpses the White Horse

at fifteen he deliberates
   lets the dust slap his face
a curl plastered to his forehead
   dark whorl on a blank slate
he watches his hands tremble
like a voyeur to his own destruction
a buttoned-up marionette holding a sheath of hot metal
   what do you have for breakfast
on the day you attempt to hurl your body
   under the legs of history?

he will fail where others succeed
   miss the shot
miss the bulbous target of a dictator's head
   consumed by the fray
of hooves & bodyguards
   he will finally know what it means
to throw yourself in front of the barrel
   of a country's delusions
to flood a parade with illicit innocence
   an officer will drag him forward
a crowd will tear his small body apart

  the boy fails
   old men rejoice
  unlike him they will die alone
   in barren kitchenettes
  from the weight of their own inaction
   their firstborn sons will wipe the brows
  of the Africa their fathers ravaged

   puberty is like an attempted assassination
  another gateway into oblivion
   spare us the terror of children
  who see right through us
  who see what little power we cling to
   & still refuse

From a Distance,
Anteo Zamboni Glimpses the Ageing Poet

the street wears the boy's name like a neon innuendo
    half a century percolates
another teenager takes aim at the officer's son
    the famed filmmaker
the lifelong poet

an intellectual's battered body kisses the trimmed grass
    of a football pitch
the suspect surrenders
    an attempted assassination is like puberty
its success sputters after a false start
    two men are left gasping in its wake
one with a ruby-encrusted gold ring
    its centre a glittering scab

the city's outskirts are scabs
    the centre is the object of our affections
the ghetto is an iron foundry
    Venice claims the word's origin for itself
the ghetto as scrapping
    a skid into a ditch of resentment
gettare is to *pour* is to *cast*
    to throw aside & encase
to incriminate the children's laughter
    seal off the contagion of their need

    the centre debases
        the ghetto erases
terraferma or target
        which wind should we stake our whole lives on
    which direction should we take
        who can we bring with us
    & who will always be left behind?

The Flower of the Thousand and One Nights

    a boy broke your heart
        you went to the desert to honour the feeling
    chosen obliteration is still chosen
        Ethiopian gold
    ancient cures for ancient afflictions
        your distractions fed you
    the Horn is a dislocation of bones
        a procession of stubborn miracles
    a dull throb felt in the gums

        black boys in white   black girls in tasselled robes
    ethereal drip   baby on hip
        girls like crescent moons   hiding by the river
    you wandered Asmara
        searching for the source
    in a stuffy office you saw her
        Lady of the Moons
    moved to tears you knew her by sight
        before you knew her
    Zumurrud   eyes like opals   exceeding definition
        you wrote the words   she repeats
    frame her telling a story   she tries to outrun

black girl on the block
    black muse beside you
your leading lady reading your script
    inhaling Isfahan's dotted gardens
the world is drunk off images
    she is a blank square for its deceptions
silver cup in hand   she bathes
    wetting her neat braids   your eyes follow
your mirrored fate   her misfortune
    soon the Pelagie Islands
will become tragedies
    for her extended family of
dreamers   & runaways

across the wedge of both Yemens
    you turn her into an ornament
an elemental beauty in the valley of origins
    in Hadramout   she is a market display
a trophy selecting her winner
    He's the one I want as my master because he has lovely eyes
the dub is strangled   an accented account
    of the choices she has
the choices we have been reduced to

you threw a cord across the water
    a lash of friendship
you loved Calabria
    wanted to share it with its victims
wanted your beloved victims to love one another
    translated Senghor by candlelight
kissed the blue fingers of his Sheba
    nine nights   & nine days
your dreams are the morning's wrinkled thoughts

Rosarno now spits out Africans
    hunts them by night
refugeehood is one of Dante's circular hells
    the priest tells the journalist
reporting for a paper I hate-read to stay informed
    on my blood-spattered hands
another translation lost in the waters
    I think of you meeting your tribe
wearing a leather jacket   the colour of prodigal soil
    standing on Mount Etna
between two volatile plates   African & Eurasian
    unashamedly dramatic in your thirst
trying to convince yourself that
    the south is the south is the south

Postcard from Castelporziano: Rare Scenes of a Poet Caught in a State of Glorified Impotence

twenty-two poets
three days
riots have needed fewer ingredients
alchemical gathering
on the beach where Pasolini was shot
Ostia's crushed nose
Africa! my only alternative
they remember him for who he was
he loved the way a foreigner does
from a burning distance
the way a son loves a father returning from a war
waged in a land his son mystifies
like the eyes of Sékou Touré
black just as Rimbaud was blond
wild spirits in polka-dot bikinis
come up for air

money is your god
the poet chants
few things the crowd claps for
they roar disgust
mosh-pit jeers
thrown chairs
bare-chested men booing
it's 1979
so the revolution is somewhere between a redacted word
& a TV advert
it's sand blowing through hair
a toothpick between Baraka's lips
it's Yevtushenko talking his big game
Ginsberg tries to pacify with lusty *oms*
for once no one listens to the North Americans
alhamdulillah

fire-breathers snatch attention
young anarchists invade podiums
promising soup for everyone
one drop makes the whole world kin
Anne Waldman wants to know what happened
to Augustine & his mother in Ostia
a man flashes the crowd
Bacchus in a bathrobe
fanculo fanculo fanculo
vim-voiced Aldo Piromalli repeats
sounding like an aunt's long-distance complaints
heartsick for her hometown
her boys in their hometowns
children pull cords
swallow mics
I think of how we need more toddler hecklers at poetry readings
more children pointing
at naked emperors

Gregory Corso, where are you?
I can't spot Ted Joans, but I know he died broke
like most Black poets
after they killed Amadou
he swore he'd never live in America again
take the hint & extrapolate
or expatriate
both involve a stretching of the body
beyond its brink

carefree sunbathers lounge
by the harbour
no one cares what the poets say
or who their poems are dedicated to
sometimes people just want
to splash about in the sun
they don't want to hear
about things they can't change
sometimes they only want to use their hands
to swim or to destroy

1960

Italian Somalia and British Somaliland reunite to form the independent Somali republic.

    The White Star is raised. The dervishes are honoured.

        La Grande Somalia is a bated breath.

            The Scramble for Africa births the scramble for a new story.

Preludes

I met you through anecdotes. An inventory of phrases
ringing in your grandchildren's ears. You were a learned man,
they said. The proverbs were yours, then ours, to receive with rolled eyes.
In all your mastered tongues, you disciplined us beyond the grave.
Your loot of ancient romances. Amharic, Yemen's brick-red Arabic,
a coastal, Swahili-peppered lilt.

Cuffed Russian & the Italian boot. A sprouting at the forked root
of sons & daughters thrown into different schools, into competing allegiances.
You chose your children's paths, sent them off to stay up all night.
Beside gas lamps, they strained over schoolwork on park benches.
Gossiped under the blank gaze of founding fathers, hammers & sickles,
the Sayid on his horse. Big, lumbering logs of men adorning posters,

their brows lifted & luminous like Egyptian starlets of a golden age.
I never met you. You, or the men whose words I read in translation.
Your life passed through mine in translation. Their love, like yours,
is irredentist. Unbothered with how heavy it weighs on its beloved's neck.
It wants more territory than it can hold. Pyrrhic parcel of want.
We are rags to be wrung by our men.
They gift us their dying. Outlive what they can.
Leave us entire worlds to bury.

An Age Until Lunch Break, An Agony at Mogadishu's Gamal Abdel Nasser School

Counting down the long fingernail of noon,
she is a bud. Hushed notes smuggled under tables
carry an urgency she will spend the rest of her life chasing.
Outside the classroom, dissonance flourishes
like shrubbery, like man-made misery.
Inside, she sits somewhere in the middle,
uncontainable as the Alps, leaning
over her assigned corner, blotting a textbook with borrowed ink.
Iskandariyah-born teacher snaps chalk in half.
Leads with love, with paternal affections.
Moon-eyed barn of bored children.
A shared rummage of pan-African hangovers.
This place is a fog.
Already dissipating.

Someday, she will be someone's mother.
Someone else's undoing.
In the retelling, she recites poetry by heart.
Learns to count backwards, starting with timelines of liberation
pinned to walls, these independence days
she will grow to see as anniversaries of customary heartbreak,
of what could have been,
of what was never allowed to bloom.

Gradations

Above the city, a stone-throwing boy is raised.
They said no sky on earth was as cloudless as ours.
None as blue.
Two leopards wag their tongues.
A shield of gold between them.
Another luminous lie.

Summon the Golden Age through the rose-tinted filter
of its inheritors.
Describe the shade of your ache.
Who does an age belong to?
Whose brooch once winked in the sun?
Whose children sheltered under a nation's promise?
Who was close, and who was closer?

Who was left squinting, with nothing
but the ink of a flag staining their fingertips?
An inventory of half-remembered songs.
Who lost so little, having already had
so little to lose?

On Memory as Molasses as Muscle as Miasma

in the old country Khadija drives a Fiat Mirafiori
full-bellied & often faulty
gas from each of its mouths   like a preacher
a cassette case lies gutted   in the glovebox
sets scratchy funk to motion
brakes grunt between her legs   she is an educated woman
the first to leave & begin elsewhere
watch her catholic schoolgirl dreams ripen
her mother is older than her own country
to be a child of such fictions is to live   fossilised in amber
look   how well she wears these myths
of borders & beginnings   like silk shawls
somewhere between a minaret   & the Arch of Umberto
fascism is just another bridge you innocently walk under
here   in this lamented age   before Kasarani
before Lampedusa   before collapse & containment
before diaspora & dispersal   before the Mediterranean claimed us as
                                                her favourites
before the burst of waters & bonds

each morning she dabs her wrists   with a drop of lilac
invents a regime of her own
at their houses she wipes a table clear   adjusts her apron
on hands and knees   she reaches the furthest crevices

fluffs one pillow after another   the weight of a silvered tray
                                  & an officer's hand
is a daily calculation   sublimate desperation into a wisp of faith
akhirah is the afterbirth   is the afterlife
is the handprint of absence   the officer's hand is the silvered tray
the silvered tray is the officer's hand   both rest warm
against the chest   both feed cousins back in the village
she dreams of return   does not know what she will return to

Napoli sighs outside   efficient in its alienation
housewives fling their windows open
eat from the morning's palms   let the breeze swell
let it usher in the kind of promises
                                a stranger can believe in

You Will Never Tell Your Daughters

what happened, or who it happened to.
You decide this, even in the moment's delayed drag,
in the sequined familiarity of your sandals.
Insist on forgetting, on destroying the satin record
of your missteps. The moon is a split lip,
spilling all over your brown shoulders.
A wash of light claims your mouth.
Agnano is hills and hunger.
From your bedroom, you can see the hippodrome.
A verdant blanket.
Almost worth all this ruin.
In years to come, the solid history of your earrings will survive.
For now, you are still young, and they graze your cheeks.
Two molten rivers, fluent in the language
of descent, reflecting the molecular weight of anguish
on your face.

You Will Deny It All

of course, beginning with the rubber band
of your diaphragm, the yielding hollow
of your desire, dilating. Blown bulb
of fire. How you once wore your contradictions
as lightly as your scarves.
Your troupe of lost sisters finding each other,
when not avoiding one another,
for fear of witnessing another woman's lack
of means or motives,
of what she has been forced to become.
Ignoring the hisses of men
whose fleshy smiles betray violent attentions.
'*Faccetta Nera*'
We shall give you another law and another king.
Keep walking. Don't stop for a second,
for a cigarette.
Africanella.
Madam. *Madamato.*
The sons of blackshirts sing of little black faces.
An abyss by the drain, a hell by the water.
Little Abyssinian, we will take you to Rome, freed.
The policemen are the worst.
They follow, draped in smoke.
They do not stop.

You Will Heave Your Body

into the cover of hallways, into crammed cafés
& impromptu gatherings, into corridors where faces
like yours recede from shadows, shed their masks,
shrug off their studied humiliation. Into hazy rooms
you will scurry, where oil stains Tupperware
& the men are rough in a language you both share.
Where they touch your waist as they pass paper plates.
Promise you the world as if they have a right to it.

1977? / 1987? / 1991?

Exodus. Refugees & returnees cross the Ethiopian-Somali frontier.

The Ogaden War is Cassandra. The Civil War is Agamemnon's bed.

Yearly, the rot intensifies. Eventually, the limb disintegrates.

Mass displacement unites the masses. Diaspora swells into millions.

Procession

long-tailed drought
follows war
war follows
long-tailed drought
like a panting dog
unable to shake off its fleas
states of emergency
states of exception
a miracle is any sweep of earth
we haven't had to abandon
a home we can carry
on our backs
bit by bit
one by one
a bootful of water
until we empty the ocean
of our sins
we who will always
on some level
believe we did something
to deserve this

Later

they said he was one of the ringleaders chased the women into the masjid army trucks ribboned the coast neighbours looked away gave their children the gift of bigger bedrooms looted their former friends they said he rested on the steps of the low building wiped their tears from his knuckles upon rising they said his legs gave out from under him a flailing he could not explain a reckoning they repeated across waters they believed what they wanted to believe that the soil never forgets that even beggars reach out with one hand atone with the other a musalla choked with howls a reddening sky the bolted windows the blemished sanctity of coral stone the tyranny of unmarked graves the enclosure of state of statelessness the enclosure of family they blamed themselves they said the people deserved divine judgement they swallowed their unruly adolescence they cursed continuity with dry tongues disavowed what they could not burn burned what they could not disavow waited until it was safe enough to look back

                                                            they are still waiting

Wink Wink

this time it happened
cascade of iced tea
then a line
hot spray of bullets &
in less than thirty minutes we
lose twenty of our children
tears a bursting sun
a feed a timeline
& every other way
into character limits
check phone
& glass screen
for condolences
unticked messages
amber tinge of panic
fifteen minutes
approximate
where you do not know
or not
his luck respectively
he deploys it with no sense

after evening prayer
& sugared straws
break
reverb &
they the land
a car is rammed into a restaurant
into a woman's back then
a breaking story
the unmournable are condensed
pulled inwards
through mist
WhatsApp now an arena
sneakers & telephone wires
like a hand to the hob
your father will reply in
a hitched breath
a fifteen-minute window
if he is still alive
he will thank god &
the wink emoji is his favourite
of irony

this time it isn't him
forgive me for always

this time it's someone else
wanting it to be someone else

Iqama

> *connoting (a) the second call to Muslim prayer, after the* adhan
> *(b) residency permit or identity documentation for foreign nationals*

been staring at the end for so long it's a beginning
been both the call to prayer
& a permit paper
been NIDO milk powder mixed with water
been the rosary beads of a dying man
been loose change made looser
been who I need to be which is exactly who I am not
been the first scent of petrol
been the first blister of love
been at the centre of a global conspiracy I want no part of
been too good for my own good
been too bad at being bad
been a sack of nectarines sliced to the sour heart
been the juice licked off a forearm
been the evidence
been the lack of evidence
been the crime scene of dreams
been the murderous practices of civility
been an avatar for apology
been a manifesto for the disenchanted
been the history of my own neglect
been too heavy with history
been the deliverance from myself
been the mind in the gutter
been the body that joins it
been the done to
been the undoing
been both the complete absence
& the presence of too much too soon

This Little, This Late

Ageing, you are closer to leaving me.
Still born early enough to have tasted it.
Drenched in the accident of your birth, the blessing
of perfect timing, you wandered your city's tree-lined streets.
Inhaled sharp breathfuls of bougainvillea. Not a year too late.
I know this means you will be taken from me sooner.

Still wouldn't have it any other way.
You lived the childhood you could never give me.
A lifetime too late, I sat between your legs.
Slathering my curls with olive oil, you unspooled
the reels of your youth. Spaghetti westerns at Cinema Nasar.
I craved your cellular memory of the Indian Ocean.

The night air licking your clavicles.
A fountain to dip your elbows in.
Old men combing their henna-stained beards.
Gentle Barbarossas clucking their tongues outside Café Nazionale.
One day, you flipped your pillow to its cold side.
Woke up. In an instant, that country was gone.

Mother, let me mourn what I have never seen.
Rub my scalp and tell me who I could have been.
Feed me a morsel or two. This hunger terrifies me.
My feet are wet. My heart is a squeeze of envy.
Thumbprints only muddy the sleeves of a family album.
I would die to relive even the most ordinary of your days.

Untitled

hooyo says if she had stayed they would have killed her

if: a suspended sentence. conversation killer. everything between then & now is all filler. fodder. unceasing intrusion, this looping afterthought with a bitter aftertaste. this thorny hedge. her children will chew on its single syllable. *if* will be their revolving universe, the ball rolling underfoot, the substance of their nightly terrors. *if* we had never left. *if* we had never come here. *if* our boys had never stepped foot in this place. *if* counts her options. opposite the Irish pub, that old abode of undercover coppers, *if* invents possibilities of her own. *if* takes a long walk, the long way home.

they: denomination of unfriendly neighbours. *they* the dictators, fanatics, frenemies, love rivals, boys next door, warlords, colleagues & various historical ghosts. home office demands its consistent narrative of cartoon villains. whole lotta *theys* & not enough time to count them. *they* the people *they* the running *they* the country.

stay: refugees are born with object permanence. few things can be counted on to *stay* still long enough to be named. the length of each *stay* is undetermined. Dadaab, Damascus, a school-sized Danish village where children followed the new arrivals, convinced they hid animal tails under their coats. *stay*? proof of residence, of a bedraggled floor to call your own. *stay* put. *stay* behind so someone else can go.

stay ready (so you don't have to get ready).

Sufficiently Memorable Password Recovery Questions for the Refugee Parent

1. Think of a street from your childhood. If it still exists, name it.

2. What was the first nickname you lost?

3. Define love as something other than duty.

4. Here is a welcome mat. You only get one word. What will it be?

5. Recall the shade of your former best friend's favourite lipstick.

6. Define the approximate shape of your rage.

7. Name the city where you first followed a man into a graveyard. Willingly.

8. Did you want to be a muse or was that something else your children decided for you?

9. When will you stop holding your breath?

10. In 11 to 15 characters, with at least one upper-case character, one number and one symbol, was it all worth it?

Year Zero

Choose your own moment of inception. Diaspora is durational loss.

We keep moving and moving and moving.

We never arrive.

Fledglings

attempt (one)

A coin toss. Two birds. Two tides of acclimation. Two heads. Two kinds of newcomers. One hurtles, encased in high-strength aluminium. A suitcase stuffed with advantages. Joins the rest. Empty-handed, though rolled sleeves have a way of betraying easier beginnings. This group bleeds redemption. Spells out a Five-Year Plan at the intermediate-level English class. They are the spangled success story. Spit-shined exceptions. They dribble lighter fluid and ambition. They will earn their wings. Earn their keep in bleached suburbs, in fist-sized towns & strip mall sprawls. Their children will blame them for all the wrong reasons. For not passing on a mythology of lack. For throwing them down the endless well of aspiration. Some will call them models. Some will call them mannequins. Like their new neighbours, they will have trouble sleeping.

attempt (redux)

Two birds. One in the bush. Is bush. Fresh off the boat. Never docking. Never quite landing. Sunny-side up. They inherit a lifetime of perpetual crisis management. Movement is fractal, maddeningly lateral. Their survival is a muzzled conspiracy. Their dying is a muzzled conspiracy. They will disappoint their children. Their taste in china will always be gauche. They are workers of no distinction, of no ascendant direction. Fixed stars by which the rest of us may determine our own positions. Their accents will always be charmless. They possess an intimate knowledge of the nation's sudden bowel movements. They are possessed. Like seers, they will not be believed. Occupying the lower rungs of citizenship's mercurial ladder, they rinse shit from bedsheets, warm the hands of elders, wipe spittle as it collects at the corners of gasping mouths. They ferry the heartbroken to & from weekend vigils. Prod squealing pigs with stun guns. Return the departed to the gutted earth.

One bird knows its nest better than the other.

                    One bird soars & another shivers in your hands.

Fluke by Any Other Name is a Flight Number

when they first came over nobody knew what Finland was or where it was or what to even wear on the flight you passed the medical examination & stood there glorious as a beggar as the Amreekan doctor laughed after the HIV test & said *you're good to go* next thing you know frost knocks wind from chests & they're in Tampere home of the swollen-bellied & coincidentally where on a crisp December mid-morning much like the day of their arrival Lenin first met Stalin at a Bolshevik conference which is neither here nor there but more pressingly is not where they would rather be if given the choice which is unlikely considering the oceanic gulf between choice & options between affection & affect put another way on arrival they still couldn't locate their new home on a map Finnair could only do so much despite regularly being ranked as one of the safest operating airlines with its last fatal accident occurring in 1963 the year of Diet Coke & four little girls & Malcolm's body in Michigan his spirit in Bandung in Nairobi in Paris in Saigon *don't be shocked when I say I was in prison you're still in prison that's what America means prison* oh for such delicious clarity the warm butter of his rage a speech later sampled by Public Enemy then recycled as part of the soundtrack to the video game *Sonic Rush* a cobalt blue & white hedgehog the same colour as the Finnish flag a force unable to catch up with itself the perfect metaphor for modernity & the ache of a wrist held in anticipation for the conveyer belt to return their luggage if not their country both will do both they carry on their shoulders

                                                        but only one will weigh them down

I Scream, You Scream, We All Scream for Ice Cream

1990. Entry point: Heathrow. Two boys.
No other way out. Handed yourself in.
Asylum-seeker. New name to get used to.
New weather to complain about.
London is a fresh calamity.
A life without cardamom in your tea is not one worth living.
Welcome to the desperate gloss of discount stores.
The burden of Bakewell tarts.
Our great land. Very green. Extremely pleasant.

You escaped into recession & riots.
Into detonated towers & Irish accents
turned away at the door. More was to come.
Imported rugs & kids going cunch.
England will always keep you guessing.
In your head, your bags are still packed.

Dreamland! Your torments are so prosaic.
Cynicism turns us into locals.
Our dreams will soon be entirely monolingual.
Turn the heating off.
We're not made of money.
We weren't made to endure either.
On the FM, a pop star crumples your expectations.
An insect shattered under a heel.
Her skull is a ballpoint pen.
She sings of Madame George & bleeding roses.
What it means to dig your own grave.
You won't know until you know it in your bones.
You wish she would shut up.

Never perfectly suited, you made the best of it.
Came with nothing and still have nothing to show for it.
Your patience is adhesive.
Your children will grow up to appreciate arthouse films.
They will pay to not understand what is going on.
A fair trade. A brilliant exchange.

Skint. Overworked. Lavish laughter.
Heavy plastic bags dig grooves into hands.
Minnow boiling in the soup of luxury real estate.
Everywhere, an argument wages about you, around you.
Your pain is agreed upon like ice cream on a hot day.
Small joys and smaller mercies.
You are trying to survive the clutter of a life you chose without choice.
You will get so good at this, you won't even notice the bruises.

Brief Dialogue Between the Self-declared East African Micronations of Regent Park Estate (Toronto) & Regent's Park Estate (London)

There is always someone to stay with.
Someone who will give up their bed,
the plushness of their comfort.
Neighbours bring pouchfuls of spices
back from the motherland. Sit without invitation.
Someone offers the heat of their body.
Willingly loses long hours to gossip.

                        Gossip slides down bannisters.
                        Legs to head. Haphazardly thrown slippers.
                        We lie in pairs like skinned kippers.
                        Against my back, your elbow is a fence.
                        Non sibi sed toti. Separation is distal.
                        Misplacement volleys between us.
                        Video chat. Background chatter.
                        All hundred, peeled eyes. Our block's
                        windows blink like an advent calendar.
                        All-seeing Argus. Our bereft, blitzed tower.
                        Our cherished nook of experience.

Experience is straddled. Like our knees hugging
the cold frame of orange benches.
I crossed an ocean to meet you here,
in your other life, so faintly similar
to my own. A meniscus between decisions
we had no hand in. Choices determining
how far apart we sit today. Our likeness
is viscous, discreetly trapped in our saliva.
Over subway rattle, I can barely hear you conspire.

                              Conspire to survive their revitalisations.
                              Teenagers hotboxing in cars, trading
                              contraband dreams in different accents but
                              similar twangs, courtesy of Xamayca,
                              insolent island of outsized brilliance.
                              Past the school gates, the leisure centre,
                              the shelter for 'Aboriginal' men,
                              throughfares tingle with familiarity,
                              the same British names flinging
                              our lives into different orbits.

Orbit the hood's circumference.
Your blood knows its way around.
Around us finance capital belches
its nuclear shrooms. Scatters ash over our heads.
How formless our dreams have become,
are becoming. Like steam rising
from a nearby church. An airless prayer.

Übertragung

Love is a Western Union transfer, or rather,
the kneaded bread it buys, the counterfeit medicine,
ruffled schoolbooks, a leg of lamb shared between seven.
Dahabshiil. World Remit. Transactional webs of need.
Be my wire of violent reciprocations.
Each trip, each tap & click, strangles like a velvet grip,
like the twin ropes of World Bank & IMF,
more pitiless abbreviations widening the gap,
this rupture of experience,
between you & I.

At the counter, I identify myself as kin.
Offer the official proof of our separation:
Her Majesty's Passport.
I am aware of what you give me.
This slick smudge of authenticity, my hangdog
ammunition, my territorial discomforts.
This poem you never wanted.
I am a smear of cushioned guilt.
My angst is a signed assault on paper.
I pay to be absolved.
Across the line, I pray you hate me less,
or for better reasons.

We speak. Your assumptions grate.
To you, my life is a lottery of possibilities.
A breeze of routine fulfilment.
Who will rob you of your innocence?
Who will break the news gently?
Show you my own throttled hopes?
Who can name it all & stand to tell the truth of it?
We are still waiting for our lives to begin here.
Our children lick their wrists in holding cells.
Here, in the land of plenty, of neat hedges
& lethal misrecognition.
We have made our fortunes.
We have lost our faces.
You begrudge me a dream that died upon arrival.
One of us is kneeling.
The other is begging.
Hard to tell the difference.
Harder still to live it.

The Apocalypse Will Taste Like Concentrated Grape Juice

Those days madrassa meant a room above the café. No chairs. Giggled conspiracies. Sizzled fat to perfume the conversation of men too long in the tooth for niceties. They had no indoor voices. We impersonated the shimmy of the Indian Ocean. A cypher perfected by the baton of the macalin's stick ruler. Counting down until the break. Until our ritual of grape-juice boxes & smuggled chocolate. We sat on our hind legs like the sun outside the dirty windows. Stained our front teeth with Shani & everything else as imported & pigmented as we were. Doomsday gossip. We swapped the coming signs. How we were taught the world would end. All the major & minor undoings. How the Hour would fall when Bedouins constructed the tallest buildings. We'd been to Dubai that one hot summer & seen this for our young selves. Drew parallels on each other's palms. Signs like the blinking of years, winters that would feel like summers, the sun's agonising rise from the west. We wanted a glorious ending. We wanted a movie. We dreamed of a finale to freeze the blood. Each day we'd wake to someone's world ending. As sure as taxes & betrayal, we saw our parents & their parents take their cues from the planet & grow indifferent to their own bodies. Too young to understand hooded men balanced on boxes or poverty's slick-talking jaw, we still knew. The world is a howl. This conclusion drawn from the quantitative analysis of playground spite, imposed bedtimes & the dread of accidentally walking into our mothers' silent sobs. Blues sprinkled like rice at a wedding. Born into & out of wandering. Collapse was our way of standing still. Is it selfish to want the world to feel your pain too? To blister the way you do? Forgive the children for their jagged dreams. Forgive those so young & so over it already. They do not mean what they say when they say they will play in the upturned soil of a split earth. When they dream of tickling the Beast behind its perky ears. They will ride its back down down down into a land of worms & warmth. Into the only place that will receive them as esteemed guests. As homecoming. As family.

The Polyphonic Urgencies of Paltalk 2.0

We're strangers here.
Youngest cusping teens. A few edging their thirties.
Uniform in our loneliness, we log on.
Find each other in the crevices of cyberspace.
Drop our cloaks of virtue.
Dial-up is a leaking valve. Webcam disconnects.
We are patient & long-suffering, like an entrepreneurial uncle
in the anachronistic ruins of his internet café.
Pass the baton of conversation.
A pipe between the lips.
Afro-puffs in a daffodil-spattered shirt. Velour.
G-Unit trackies in chlorophyll green.
A/S/L. Chat is duck & dash.
Here, boredom is honoured.
RE4LNi99A4Lyfe types from Norway.
Replies to his gags come hours later, courtesy of Nairobi's shaky connection.
Someone is explaining the Canadian school system.
Someone is quoting Tupac.
Someone is quoting the Prophet.
Though we are scattered, we circle the same rooms.
Our split selves mingle in the veins of undersea cables,
meeting each other on LCD screens.
We reassemble the fragments we have become.

A Violet Coagulation of Dispersals

I

All the real niggas are dead or in prison. We are elaborating gently. We are gooey in the middle. The distance between those twin possibilities is Cartesian. We know they will kill us, in small & flagrant ways. Still, we follow breadcrumbs & hope for a dignified annihilation. Slippery as newborn calves, we glisten. We are fighting for the inalienable right to be ugly & still have an open casket. We are loud about our pain & the world hates us for it. We kill with the blunt instrument of kindness.

II

Some people are born possessive nouns. Some people leave & others stay. Amal with the soft earlobes, the suppressed lisp. Raspberry milkshakes at the park. The skin on her knees like wild chanterelles foraged at dawn. Recall the violet of her mood ring. Forever stuck on the colour of asphyxiation. *We are suspicious of purple*, Jarman wrote, *it has a hollow bombast*. We found his words in the clammy belly of a Hampstead charity shop. His purple was exhibitionism, Hendrix, impish Prince, imperial tyranny, smut, the smell of Alexander the Great's piss, luxury, a violation of decent taste. Always, a passage. Some people are drawn to the dusk of other interpretations. Easter. Funk. Failure. Christian repentance in violet robes. Away from our cluttered sadness, Jarman wields his cane, bent like a prophet-in-waiting. We are gassed-up & drunk off our own subjectivity. Terminally disappointed the way baby girls raised on prophets & rappers are bound to be. Both die young & leave behind poor imitations. We refuse to destroy ourselves to give meaning to your Order.

III

During that inching hour just before iftar, the holiest month was ushered in by IM chat sessions & notification alerts. She moved to Cairo just in time for the revolution. Like clockwork. There we go again. Blackness as centripetal force, as timekeeping beyond time, as magpie collation, as marooned miscellany, as an inventory under siege, as a mad ting, a *wahala*, a *junoon*, a reverie of blue-veined jinns, as a crush of meaning, a sodden map, a returnless edge, a stutter of absence. Satellite beams marble & cubic zirconia & televised coverage of millions breaking their fasts courtesy of the Saudi government-run station. Yaa Allah, do not impose on us one who does not have mercy on us, one who does not fear You. The centre withholding again. Like when Muna's sister left for medical school in Damascus, only for the war to start & she told everyone she didn't get this far just to leave without graduating & her aabo said he didn't give a shit if a bomb fell on her head she was going to be a doctor otherwise what was the point of trekking ten days on his feet to reach the Kenyan border? We wished her what we could. Well.

IV

Yusra in Al-Rehab City. Me in Blighty. They tried to make me go to Al-Rehab, I said, No, no, no. Prepaid calling card just to make that dead joke. The first among many. Amal? She left. Maryam too. Nasra & Iman. All gone. All specialists in the art of errantry. Egypt is like mandatory military service for the likes of us. We all gotta do our time. Tahya Masr! There will be other arrivals, other disintegrations, to come. You won't know it until you do. Let this be the fragmented measure of our exquisitely accumulated realness. Realness as quantified by the lusciously clandestine currency of struggle, whatever that means to whoever is asking. I love you like I love each & every one of my girls, my Xalimos & Xayaats & Xanaans, full-throated, helicopter-pad, pulmonic-sourced, slave-name substitute, irritant-hazard-symbolled, cryptic, antepenultimate, decennial dolls. We are the vectors of our own beginnings. Neither former nor latter, we sing of the blood-borne dispossession, the night sweats, the tactile touch, the nevermore thereafters, the heart's knock-kneed double dutch.

V

Here's to all the demoralised duplicates. The scale of your horror is Homeric. Who else can strut without destination, without the slightest inclination to believe in what is said about you? This cheap pocket mirror is all the reflection you need. Everything else bears the flatness of chronology. Bask. Look behind your shoulder. What did they leave you with? This gush of continuity errors. This skipping record. Understudy for a role you will never inhabit. Your grandmother's mole, like your father's status, skipped a generation. Let bitterness drizzle over you. Somewhere, in some other wafer-thin slice of reality, your dreams are pillowed. You are middle class & sleekly Afropolitan. An ingénue sucking the sap of state corruption off your fingers. You are a kitten-heeled Mogadishu ⇌ Rome-shuttler. A well-bred hustler. Street kids shine your shoes and you will still think you are innocent. Buckle in the present. Count your blessings. For camels passing through the eyes of needles. For being born two decades too late for the fluff of such fantasies. For your clean hands. Occupy the here & now, in loud-mouthed Midwestern skin, shaking slush from boots. Or supple against the spine of a wheezing Europe. In pufferjacketed Rinkeby glory. Baptised in the public waters of North London lidos. In landless love.

Balcony Dispatches, 2002

All is background noise.
I am barefoot, browning my arms on the edge,
awaiting the mandated collapse of afternoon siestas.
I am watching myself watch the old women below,
clicking their heels against uneven pavements,
carrying bags and gossip.
Unlike so much else, their habits are reliable.
Their black plastic bags filled with grapes.
A glut of green.

All is abandoned dreams.
A dictator's wisdoms painted stark on walls.
We are not free but we have found a place to catch our breath.
That means something. Or at least, it must.
Like grapes, our neighbourhoods are clusters,
on top and up against each other.
Through bloodied fellowship, each distant brother
gives the other a bed, a foldable mattress
to lay another head.

We arrive in cycles, in waves of degradation.
One after the next. Take turns baby-sitting.
We listen to Asmahan on the radio and finger our wounds.
Us children are scattershot.
Scrap in playgrounds in a language we half-know.
In the Old City, we simulate drowning.
No one can tell us where we'll be in a year's time.
We are becoming self-taught in the art of disappearance.
We don't know what we want because we've never had it.

I walk with my father, dripping rose ice cream.
Masākin Barzah, I remember your canisters of laughter.
I remember the old women pinching my cheeks.
I remember the dead cat flattened by speeding boys.
The cat is in another age and you are in another age.

Ice-cream vendor, I'm sorry for laughing at your joke before you told it.
Father, I'm sorry for not being a worthwhile sacrifice.
Damascus, I'm sorry we can't meet again.

2003–present

The Year of Return. The child catches sight of the homeland.

    The poet glorifies what the local dreams of escaping.

        How many graves will you disturb with your longing?

First Sight

A part has come to find itself.
Whatever that means.
A part wants to catch sight of a dying relative.
A part wants to film the dying.
A part needs a husband or wife.
They make them better back home.
A certain desperation that can't be store-bought
Ferments in places like these.
A part needs to feel needed. A part takes its seat.
A part fastens its belt.
A part prepares for landing.

The last part has come to see for itself if
the needle will finally find its north,
bend the body into prostration.
If the lips will recognise the soil they press against.
If everything they said was true.

Landing

(An erasure indebted to Gwendolyn Brooks)

you did not know

        Afrika

you

    did not know

        the   continent

      reached

   you

I could not   come
      over

  come

     Black

somewhere

  You would not have believed

       meeting you

Landing

```
the heat              the road

my            belief

            thanked        me

          Some
          places

        though drowsy    unwillingly

  dissonant and
                      done   done   done
```

Delete as Appropriate

it was the first / final summer

the first time I returned / left

there were no direct flights / questions

we went the long / only way

the heat welcomed / punished us

the first kiss upon arrival / departure

grandmother recognised / never forgot the marketplace

her body finally leapt into movement / life

I followed / failed her

I was swallowed by a mob of family / strangers

everyone could tell I was / wasn't from there

they said it was the way I walked / sat

I tripped over my own words / intentions

I knew nothing / enough

The Plural Possible

'I hear you talkin' 'bout "we" a lot – oh, you speak French now?'

—PartyNextDoor

Past the Greek Orthodox church, we linger down streets named after martyrs. Google Maps is thankfully useless. From Avenue du Ghana to Boulevard du 9 Avril 1938. The smell of fried potatoes clings to the skin of nostrils. Old Medina engulfs. Detours to follow, detours to forego. A being-together that welcomes the uncertainty of a false step. If there's no definable entrance or exit, you can't get lost. Loss loses meaning. Track your way in teahouses. Hissing oil vies with the sounds of Miriam Makeba's daughter asking us if we remember Malcolm, if we remember what it meant to wake up Black & alive & free in Algiers. The long 20th century rattles like a coin in a cup. Let us avoid the puddles of its failures. Crisp apple & mint. Pass the pipe clockwise. So much of it all depends on how, not what, we remember. Owl-eyed men sweep doorsteps. The Sahel remains securitised. Dispossession has to be more than an icebreaker. Kinship more than the kindling of decolonial lullabies. We are trying to be responsible with our pain. The coast will not let us forget it. A cab ride away, time belongs to plastic debris & giggling schoolgirls. Sunburnt expats turn suburbs into playgrounds. Approach where Fanon once shared bread with howling fighters. Like all children of Manichean nightmares, he worked but barely slept. At the hospital, they called him the Black Doctor. There were other names, some less polite. All closer to some kind of truth. What are a few words between bloodied brothers? *The blood of the Maghreb is sufficiently generous.* Massacred villages jostle for space in his footnotes. Some of us will spend a lifetime competing for the acknowledgement of wounds.

We are together for better & for worse. Fanon's cavernous *We*, the *We* of the Algerian, the Martinican, the exiled South African mother, the Sahrawi guerrilla, the Somali teenager in the Libyan prison camp. Fanon's *We* had the capacity to contain them. His colleagues believed in a *We* too shrunken for reciprocity. Politics is a parsing of the *We*, the maintenance of its enclosure/s, the engulfment of all who attempt to defy its confines. Territory as terror. The plural personal is the evidence of murderous affinity. It is always an absence. Who is betrayed by every assumed *We*?

Later, we trade bad jokes & olives on the roof. Children of rural southerners & seasoned hustlers recount nascent revolutions. Trigger-happy snipers, toppled despots & embittered survivors; theirs is a revolving cast of characters. The fortunate ones can afford to exchange one banlieue for another. Distant cousins are both blueprints & harbingers. Nostalgia is bidirectional. Vantage point makes all the difference. Africa becomes a repository of unceasing fantasies, the sublimation of our curdled angst. It does not move. Not until we move over it, or back to it. Self-deception is an occupational hazard of returnee life. Here, the soda is a radioactive orange. After dark, we will grill chicken & discuss the lapsarian nature of failure. We are trying to disentangle the *We*, to test its dimensions, to scuff our shoes against its brittle edges. This will feel like a kind of death. *A death on the job site, a death at the movies*. People like us are dying anyway. People like us, but not us. Daily, the distinction collapses even as it establishes itself.

        I don't want to guard something I don't own.

Apricot Season

Evening. A hung net of desire.
We made a feast out of survivor's guilt.
No incoming messages.
You translated and I listened.
My shirt was a lilac mistake.
I struck at the heart of the matter,
inevitably finding your cheek.
A rough target for my fantasies of permanence.
Carthage was a ruin behind us.
The desert was a ruin of our own choosing.

Everyone thinks they're an unfulfilled genius but you actually are.
I said this out loud, and a grin split your face.
Forgiveness suffused the air.
We couldn't stand the weight of it.
I fingered the ragged edges of your grief.
Thanked you for giving me nowhere to hide from it.
Our eyes obscenely brown in the light.
Your bare legs, a life sentence.
I unpeeled myself from the passenger seat.
It was no use pretending you had not stolen my breath.
A trick requiring a hat and a shredded rabbit.
I wanted to lie down in the middle of the road and die like a rabbit.
Give me a place to put down all this feeling.
My hands are too small and untrustworthy.
The branches too heavy with apricots.

Dunyā

it's all mad in this
no reprieve in this
a rough deal in this
it is how it is in this
done out here in this
diaspora through this
just another day in this
up from the belly of this
trust in what comes after this
not ours but we persist in this
make not of us an example in this
grant us somewhere beyond this

2020

July marks the 60th anniversary. The poet is the antagonist of linearity.

    The diaspora poet is born an antagonism.

        You begin where you were told the story started.

            You keep the timer ticking.

The Native Informant Describes a Reading to Her Friends in the Ends

'Steve Biko died while I was blind drunk in London. Soweto burned while I was sunk in deep thought about an editor's rejection slip.'

— Dambudzo Marechera

It's like the story of the crow & the peacock
You are the crow
Peacocking
Like a friendly cross-examination
Like a masquerade ball of private misery
A mugshot confessional
Like tap-dancing with borrowed shoes
A backhanded stunt
Like attending your own funeral as a spectator
Like a pat on the back
For all the worst reasons
Like a party trick overstaying its welcome
Nobody wants to hear your grievances
Unless they can clap to the beat
Of your acquiescence

Righteousness is so pedestrian
Two-step
Bust a different move
Try the last and most common taboo
Being poor
It's like an electric slide
With a line-up of opps
Like being articulate
& having nothing to show for it
A bit like falling down the stairs
& mistaking the experience
for love

A Tableau of Aspiration
or
Franklin Sitting on the Solitary Garden Deckchair in 1973's
A Charlie Brown Thanksgiving

black poets strain around table / not any table / *the* Table™

                      the table in the head / the table in the courtyard

/ all flat expanse / natural oak blend / baby / the whole nine yards

                      finest linen / unfurls / a lolling tongue

all nine lives needed / to survive this napkinned jurisdiction / of personalised

                      cutlery / there aren't enough chairs / this is expected

maybe even desired / black poets dip / long / lustrous / spoons

                      into andalusian gazpacho / grief is as elegant

as soup stains / blotting the sanctity of cloth / & canon

                      palette cleanser for the dulled soul / narcotised rage

is all the rage / eat / enumerate /

black poets are sick

    of watching black people die on glitchy screens

are sick of being reminded / of all the ways / we are not

    the black people dying on glitchy screens

are sicker still / of pretending not to know the difference / dumas begs

    to differ / *what news from the black bastille?*

reporting from the trenches / to the warmongers / yes sir / yes sir

    what news from the bottom? / three bags full

pretence keeps fridges well-stocked / the landlord's incoming

    messages / at a minimum / black poets want

bigger tables / this is the bare minimum / want more / seats /

    plusher cushions / we deserve snuff films

with better resolution / we say / the dining room is a swamp

    of monomania / leaving the room / is never an option

when the room is in your head / you can never leave / court moth-balled

    microclimates of microaggressions / lament

narrow hallways / laugh at bad jokes / mourn choices made

    even as we repeat them / we are who

we break bread with / we are who we break ourselves for /

    jaws unhinge at the feet of luminaries / collect

whatever / left / falls from tables / of renowned / award-winning cowardice /

    look up to get the chance

to look down / black poets cannot convince ourselves / cannot forgive

    ourselves / for what we are about to do

become sloppy / ancestral ventriloquists / trained provocateurs

please understand / black poets are big fans

    of rights given / of frothy righteousness / of rewriting faithless accounts

        of who we are / of what we can be

gaseous / with impotent fury / we flail upwards / don't ask us

    for better excuses / we are hungry too

for what / we are undecided / meanwhile / the white poets

    have finally discovered / they are white

throw petalled confetti / jobs / second chances / at black poets

    who remind them / that they are white

that they / too / are gorgeous martyrs / outside / other black poets flee

    bright lights / receive no invitations /

black poets of dubious allegiances / spree /

    converge / into shattered mist / welcome dissolution

show out / show us up / *what news from the bureau?*

for once / no one cares / about our place settings

    the virtues of irrelevance / are lost on us / our dreams too slight

        for those black poets who want / no part of this

want every part / of everything / want more than heaving

    tables / than well-paid contortion / powdered paranoia /

hallowed hall / hallucinations / we envy this vox populi / of unlit alleyways /

    their captive audiences of chattering millions / even their enemies

are worthier / than ours / chalk fades / dividing lines / redrawn

    hot summers clarify / which black poets survive poetry /

    & which write it

A Guest Takes Off Her Shoes

> *'The city displays one face to the traveller arriving overland and a different one to him who arrives by sea.'*
>
> — Italo Calvino

Baker in Paris.
Baraka in Ostia.
Baldwin in Istanbul.
Malcolm in Jeddah.
McKay in Marrakesh.
Robeson in London.
Huey in Beirut.
Kwame's first breath of Algiers.
Here I am finally in the mother country.
Nina in Monrovia.
Nina in Nijmegen.
Nina sick of home.
Nina chronic with homesickness.
Everybody loves their niggas foreign.

Swap the Anglo bind, the squalor of the mind,
for candle-dipped café deliberation.
Storefront, salon, soirée. Jazz bar,
bazaar, ballroom, bedsit.
A sip from the municipal fountain.
Off to the races. Trattoria, port, pulpit, pedestal.
Zoot suit. Zazou.
Dinner is air & contrarianism.
High society, low stakes.
The European eats from your clenched hands.
The Arab is a slippery accomplice.
The African is a stubborn homecoming.
You are a detached appendage.
Everything is applause.
Your words flit between seated ardour.
An audience gathers, reads only the sealed envelope
of your body, the dark pulp of your symbology.

The war is elsewhere, always elsewhere.
They clap   & look away.

Everybody loves their niggas foreign.

If You Call Me Brother, Am I Yours?

Kilburn boy dons *kufi* cap
decides to go back
beleaguered
in black
though he has never been anywhere
near those three seas
one-way flight to Turkey
border inches closer
war over the shoulder
he maps out a conquest
glory to be grasped
with black hands
& black flags
end one life
to begin another
bystanders bear the brunt
of his identity crisis
of what his country did to him
of what he did to himself
the sick pleasure of false brotherhoods
a commonwealth
of chosen believers
home-grown crews
forged on the melted earth
of fleeing survivors

they said he was nothing
now he's a state
a nation of unrecognised lines an
invention like all others
what the newspapers call a *death cult*
armies of orphans
run in the opposite direction
this time
colonisers arrive with prayer beads
& kalashnikovs
their accents
thick London treacle
chickens roosting in distant nests
an outsourced heartbreak

maybe he'll come back
in one piece
or maybe not
it was not
it was not his place
to stage his tragedy
inside someone else's living room
their carpeted blood on his shoes
their love
returned like this

Muddied Commitments

for Nargis

I

the son's forehead is cool
to the touch
dust entrapped between his eyelashes
all the boy sees when he looks up
is a hooded prayer
the black shroud
he calls father
a shallow breathing against his back
their sandalled toes
pointing in the same direction
beloved in his arms
beloved Najaf's pure dirt
soil that has lapped up centuries of blood
their kingdom of barbed wire
encircles

the son won't recognise a face he can't see
behind a smog of authorised sadism
and what face could a condemned man reveal
to the child in his lap?
how would he arrange the scene of his powerlessness?
Adam was born from soil
a moulded clay slackened

by the breath of life
what can you tell a child about banishment
that war will not teach him?

small bodies wash up on beaches
or crushed under rubble
under a rain of white phosphorus
& sanctions
an unmanned hail imprints a fear of clear skies
into the hearts of schoolboys
even in our curated fury
the act of witness degrades us
we still live like the clouds
are ours alone to watch
with abandon

our mercy comes with caveats
separating wheat from chaff
men from women
adults from teenagers
teenagers from toddlers
fighting age from innocent
the deserving from the undeserving
the child from the father's lap
the father's lap from the child
diaspora is negotiating the terms of betrayal
you are alive here because they're not
over there
you are unblemished
because they are tainted with bad luck
& bad choices

II

from a distance
a Frenchman observes
a hand's arc
a stroke of hair
the sublime grace of a man
cradling his child
they are so beautiful it hurts

III

back from ziyarah
you blistered with experience
in your hands
blessed soil gathered
smuggled in your suitcase
handfuls of dirt
powdered evidence of your spirit
lit by the sight of your father's hometown
by the jagged landscape
spotted from your window-seat view
your breath a spray against glass
an exaltation

your summer was my summer
a few summers ago
though the site of our landings may have differed
we were both inching closer
to a womanhood of our own making
on the way there
you pulled out a talisman
from somewhere deep in your satchel
polythene knots of soil
traces of Najaf warmed in your hands
on a London train
held its scent to my face
asked me to inhale

I didn't know how to share
in the flood of your longing
we sat there like two kids dragging lungfuls of glue
lying dazed on the grass
hiccupping fantasies
we mourned the streets we would never play in
the homes we would never be raised in
the jokes we would never tell
in our mother tongues
to the schoolgirls we would have befriended
we would have been
we mourned the holes in our tights
the holes we were
from inside the countries which deprived us
of the countries haunting our sleep
we were learning how the world works
how it worked on us
who this *us* really was

I remember you
the way you remember that summer
that day
you taught me something about resentment
what it was & what it wasn't
love was a hooded figure
we could never turn our backs on
it was choosing which direction to face
whose face to recognise in the dark
who we forgive again & again
leaning close
I remember you
elbow to elbow
one day you said
this soil will be a witness
I promise you

Glory Be to the Gang Gang Gang

In praise of all that is honest, call upon the acrylic tips and
make a minaret out of a middle finger, gold-dipped
and counting. In the Name of Filet-O-Fish, pink lemonade,
the sweat on an upper lip, the backing swell and ache
of Abdul Basit Abdus Samad on cassette tape, a clean jump shot,
the fluff of Ashanti's sideburns, the rice left in the pot,
the calling cards and long waits, the seasonal burst
of baqalah-bought dates.

Every time they leave and come back to us alive.

Birthmarks shaped like border disputes.
Black sand. Shah Rukh's dimples, like bullets
taking our aunties back to those summer nights,
these blessings on blessings on blessings.

Give me the rub of calves,
rappers sampling jazz,
the char of frankincense
and everything else that makes sense
in a world that don't.

Akhis & Afterthoughts

What's mine is ours. I inherit your foxholes.
What to call this fizz of recognition,
this small stir of besiegement,
I see in the crush of your eyes?
I name what is between us slippage, an alternative currency.
Our festering limerence.
A wreckage of intimate proportions.

Some days, community feels like a life sentence.
I claim you for what you are.
Not what I want you to be.

Be my constellation of care, my webbed network of kith,
my siblings in estrangement, my loose tribe, even looser ummah,
qibla-facing qabiil, my lungfuls of smoke, all open-faced & seething,
each smile a scythe to the long grass of my days. I lose you in the naming.
Dread-heavy hoteps trading conspiracies & skins by the fruit & veg stalls.
The unrepentant yardies, long-bearded attar peddlers, the night bus harassers,
the gum-smacking aunties expertly folding their headwraps, the aunties
who aren't really aunties but who you'll still call aunties, in your struggle
to place their decade of arrival on their tight faces.

Lest we forget the afterthoughts of the afterthoughts,
the purple-lipped vagrants, the lost children of their children,
the paranoid breddas debating with angels, each stray straggler,
each fresh-faced hustler. The bus drivers hollering at each other
across concrete islands, the schoolgirls screwfacing me on the tube
as they share an umbilical knot of headphones. All my sweet, sweet collaborators.
Spotless socks & sandals, those white-thobed brothers welcoming Friday,
trembling with regrets, crossing a sacred threshold with their right foot first,
guarding their fresh kicks, reminding me, that yes,
religion & consumerism can live alongside each other on the same shoe shelf.
Another blood-bound contradiction.
Like family itself.

I belonged to you before I knew you.
Before I could choose to.
Horn to Harlesden to Jozi to the 6ix
to 6*th* of October to +61 & wherever else we have to run to next.
Wherever else we magnetize misfortune.
Where even the dogs look at us suspiciously.
In praise, I am protracted.
Pray we won't be as short-lived as our summers.
Pray we will find a way back to each other,
despite each other.

Bad Diaspora Poem

'Diasporism is a romance as cunning as one's homeland is.'
—R. B. Kitaj, 'First Diasporist Manifesto'

Audience demands easy answers. Wants wobbling chins & intonated quiver.
A sigh to roll through its shared body. Enter: clear devils & clearer sinners.

Heart wants what it wants. Applauds what it will. Diaspora poems as group therapy.
Cohesion takes practice. Turn on the faucet. Distribute drip-fed sincerity.

Exotic fruits bop in buckets. Sweet mangoes, pomegranates, figs.
Ripe signifiers weighing down the basket of poems such as these.

O, long grain rice! The wonders you have done for international relations.
Rajab. TRS Asia's Finest Foods. Cash & carry spice supply. Our sacred equation

of ambient smells. Lists ticked off. Turmeric, ginger, saffron, cumin, tamarind.
Honey sweetens metaphors about mother tongues we can no longer gossip in.

Bottled Zamzam water anoints blessings. Clockwise. Dead Sea cleaves.
Throw it all against the wall. Hope something sticks. Symbols sieved

through the net of our mutually assured, intimately held delusions.
Let's invent a myth we can lean on. Let's call it a community. An obligation

to uterine origins. Joint enterprise, if you will. Our fantasies come prebuilt.
Qurbajoog. Far-flung strangers, we tend to our crumbling shrines of guilt.

Be in this world as if you were a stranger, the Hadiths were quick to warn
of attachment's conceit. The estranged will inherit the earth. The scorned

will get their dues soon enough. Camus killed the true stranger on the beach.
From the corpse's perspective, diaspora is brutish absurdism. A tidal overreach.

Each faction earns its name. We are mirrored & rippling beyond confines
of time zones & postcodes. Grant us our wonky taxonomy of punchlines.

We bear our lives like bad jokes. Reer fish & chips. Ciyaal caseer. Doppelgängers
of chilly Nordic pragmatism. Little Mogadishu on the Mississippi. A grammar

of differences we liquefy and scatter, in the name of our borderless love.
In the name of our tangled, heaving body burning for want of, in need of

a patch of dirt to finally call its own. These diaspora poems are monsoons
of second-hand nostalgia. Our diluted vials of passion. Shiny heirlooms

we buff with dropped lines. Ours, all ours. A promised kingdom to claim.
Branched favour. Our fence to stake. Others to drive out, dispossess, defame

in the name of our hard-earned wounds, the oozing pity we have endured
like entombed ruins, like worthy causes. Walking reminders of an inured

past they won't let us easily forget. A present which won't let us rest.
With everything which killed us, still kills us, we are artfully enmeshed.

Qulub names the grief of a camel for its dead mate. Repurpose the word
for an absence which rarely leaves those who left. Embellish an overheard

yearning our poems can only approximate. Finger-trace the diagnosis, by way
of Lamming, courtesy of Camden's library system. *Soon as they know you*, he says,

they will destroy you. Diaspora poems want to be known. We want to be gutted
by pious mic drops & vapid priorities. Yes, our allegiances are sullied.

We are victims, which means we are innocent. Immaculate & self-possessed.
We are victims, so our poems must be good, like their subjects. Uncomplicated

in their general thrust. Our love is a fanged celebration, so greedily uncurbed
in its violent conclusions. So sure of itself. Its soil disturbingly undisturbed.

The best things in life are foregone. Take a seat. You are invited to gawk.
But always respect the hustle. This crime scene is as much ours as yours.

Like our rhymes, we harden. Horizons narrowed into slits of ambition,
into the besieged nooks of part-time nationalisms, of intense affiliations

with long gone yesterdays of no real record. Long time, no see.
Infect the host with our fever. Rejoice. Deflect with papers & degrees.

Our loyalties are dual. Send back the creamed top of our earnings, in sweat,
to inflame the wars we fled, the wars still raging, the dozen unpaid debts

of our cruel devotion. One rule for us and one rule for the native. Beyond
& exceeding nation. No b(order) can contain our skilled hypocrisy. Our bond

of resuscitated fables. We diaspora in tides & wanes, replayed sans irony.
Horrors fleeing in seven directions. Scatterings first revealed in Deuteronomy.

Babel's towers fall apart at the seams. *Maafa*s multiplied, sprinkled like prayers
in the wind. Easy come, easy go. In this dormant language, we love with our livers.

The OGs of dispersal walk amongst us. Ham's children tripping through
our churning age where the displaced displace their brothers on cue,

as the wheel slowly turns, until it's your turn. Choiceless, you are intertwined,
Diaspora poems are sackfuls of shame. Pick a bone. Pick a goldmine

of plundered experience. A tailor-made calling. We have been cursed with the duty
of memory. Meanwhile, Babylon is unbearably creative with her misery.

This lesson learnt from Rasta uncles dropping pearled wisdom on street corners.
From the captive Hebrews before them. Gratitude for reluctant philosophers

whose scarred hands slice cosmology, recounting Mussolini's bomber planes,
Ethiopian flesh spattered against trees, the long, hot nights when the rains

would not stop. Chant it down into the ground. Mutabaruka at Sunsplash
'82 threading a line from Marco Polo to Columbus to West Indies whiplash.

Genocide as glue. Diasporas held together by felled trees, by a world birthed
through the destruction of another. The luck-graced are haunted in reverse.

Our diaspora poems need no introduction. Need no determinable direction
beyond our exposed navels. Like tan-trousered Black presidents flexing

for photo ops beside the Door of No Return. Who No Go No Know.
Like kids sent back for correction, passports confiscated, a backflow

into knuckle-slap boarding school re-education. Movement is fluid.
Some will lose everything. Some do nothing but gain. The cost never is

yours alone to reckon with. Diaspora poem, be the wart by which, bleeding,
we may recognise one another. Be ceremonial. Terribly kitsch & keening.

A cheap stamp of inaugural pain. Vintage bedroom wall posters left unpeeled.
Strut of costumed fury. Plead your case in italics, even when there is no need.

We reconstruct loss with snapping fingers. Our bugbears are usual.
Mispronounced names. Growing pains. Playground alienation of predictable

velocity. Our mothers & motherlands smothered with breathless praise,
given starring roles. They suffer. They shine like glass. Their pedestals raised

into whipping posts. Laundry list of agonies we beg, borrow & steal.
Diaspora poems are phantom limbs. Bless their infinite niche appeal.

Surrender to their turn, like a brush to water. Ancestors hold the power
to upstage us. Haunt our poems. We fear their unimpressed glower.

We fear they don't think of us all. Poems are messy family reunions, at best.
Attest to everything the elders have given you. Do anything but let them rest.

Sing our people's beauty so we may desperately prove it to ourselves.
Diaspora poems are unexceptional droughts. The heart's rummaged ghazals.

Settle or be unsettled. Take the bait. World sells us false images we counter
with our own half-truths. We water these seeds together. شتات into shared banter

we wear like a second skin, like the black drama of henna-painted hands.
What's yours to claim isn't always yours to take. Kafka refused Canaan,

though it tried to swallow him. Diaspora poems are quicksand. Original sin.
A never-ending arrival. Distrust follows like a faithful dog. Suspicion

of the very place you call your own. Community is a nightly decision we make.
A huddle of kin and criminal, in common shelter. In its love, we suffocate.

Celebrate its tender mass, its skittish glances, WhatsApp groups seeking kidney
donations, its states of ecstasy & surveillance, its fading playbook. Our disunity

has a catastrophic charm. Bound by the accident of our colliding elsewheres,
in this new elsewhere. Going somewhere we don't know yet, an everywhere

of interminable retreat. We have no name for it yet. Only *soon come*.
Settle or be unsettled. Diaspora poems celebrate what can never be won.

Acknowledgements

The following poems have previously appeared in these publications:

'Reciprocity is a Two-way Street', *Poets*
'On Memory as Molasses as Muscle as Miasma', *Wasafiri*
'Wink Wink', *Queen Mob's Teahouse*
'Iqama', *DATABLEED*
'Fluke by Any Other Name is a Flight Number', and 'The Apocalypse Will Taste Like Concentrated Grape Juice', *Doing the Most with the Least*
'A Violet Coagulation of Dispersal', *The White Review*
'A Tableau of Aspiration or Franklin Sitting on the Solitary Garden Deckchair in 1973's *A Charlie Brown Thanksgiving*', *Jewish Currents*
'Glory Be to the Gang Gang Gang', *Poetry*

Notes

'Reciprocity is a Two-Way Street' includes an epigraph from Faysal Cumar Mushteeg's poem 'Ha Derderin Carrada!/Don't Strike Against the Soil!', translated by Maxamed Xasan 'Alto' and Clare Pollard published by The Poetry Translation Centre.

'From a Distance, Anteo Zamboni Glimpses the White Horse' and 'From a Distance, Anteo Zamboni Glimpses the Ageing Poet' restage two assassinations. In 1926, fifteen-year-old anarchist Anteo Zamboni fired a shot at Italy's Fascist dictator Benito Mussolini in a failed assassination attempt. The teenager was subsequently lynched by a mob. Pier Paolo Pasolini, the renowned Italian poet and filmmaker, was assassinated in November 1975. Beaten and run over by an Alfa Romeo GT (possibly his own), his body was found on the beach at Ostia.

'Postcard from Castelporziano: Rare Scenes of a Poet Caught in a State of Glorified Impotence' includes translated lines from Pasolini's poems '*Alla Francia*' and '*Frammento alla morte*', as well as Ann Waldman's poem 'Maelstrom: One Drop Makes the Whole World Kin'.

'Sufficiently Memorable Password Recovery Questions for the Refugee Parent' takes after Soheil Rezayazdi.

'Landing' is an erasure of 'To the Diaspora', a poem by Gwendolyn Brooks.

'The Plural Possible' begins with an epigraph from the PartyNextDoor's 2016 song 'Come and See Me', written by Jahron Brathwaite, Noah Shebib and Aubrey Graham. The poem also includes lines from Frantz Fanon's *Toward the African Revolution: Political Essays*, translated by Haakon Chevalier.

'A Tableau of Aspiration or Franklin Sitting on the Solitary Garden Deckchair in 1973's *A Charlie Brown Thanksgiving*' includes lines from Henry Dumas's poem 'Mosaic Harlem'. Taken from *Knees of a Natural Man: The Selected Poetry of Henry Dumas*, published by Thunder's Mouth Press, 1989.

The epigraph in 'A Guest Takes off Her Shoes' is taken from Italo Calvino's *Invisible Cities*, translated from the Italian by William Weaver, Vintage Publishing, 1997.

'Muddied Commitments' is informed by an image I saw as a child and have never forgotten: Jean-Marc Bouju's 2003 photograph of a hooded Iraqi prisoner cradling his four-year-old son at a US detention camp in Najaf, Iraq.

This book would never have been wrenched out of me if it wasn't for the insistent prodding of family, friends, mentors, accomplices and co-conspirators. You know who you are. I owe you the immeasurable. My boundless gratitude for the long, meandering conversations, the dinners cooked side by side, the spare beds, the insightful observations, the shared discomfort, the hard lessons, the tough love doled out in bursts of life-altering clarity. Even when geography separates us, when it mocks us with its arbitrary cruelties, you have been there for me, across time zones and calling codes.

Here, finally, is something for you to hold.

penguin.co.uk/vintage